BGI

9/14

PHILIP
PULLMAN

ALL ABOUT THE AUTHOR™

PHILIP PULLMAN

LAURA LA BELLA

ROSEN
PUBLISHING

New York

Published in 2014 by The Rosen Publishing Group, Inc.
29 East 21st Street, New York, NY 10010

Library of Congress Cataloging-in-Publication Data

La Bella, Laura.
Philip Pullman/Laura La Bella.—First edition.
    pages cm.—(All About the Author)
Includes bibliographical references and index.
ISBN 978-1-4777-1766-0 (library binding)
1. Pullman, Philip, 1946-—Juvenile literature. 2. Authors,
English—20th century—Biography—Juvenile literature.
I. Title.
PR6066.U44Z74 2014
823'.914—dc23
[B]
                                                    2013011258

Manufactured in the United States of America

CPSIA Compliance Information: Batch #W14YA: For further information, contact Rosen Publishing, New York,
New York, at 1-800-237-9932.

CONTENTS

Lyra Belacqua and Will Parry journey through parallel universes with armored polar bears, magical devices, witches, and daemons.

A motley crew of children fights crime on the streets of Victorian London.

Sally Lockhart searches for answers after she receives a mysterious letter following her father's death.

Over the course of a summer, Ginny Howard learns family secrets that change everything she knows about her family.

This is the world of Philip Pullman. It's a place where mystery meets intrigue, where romance blossoms, and where children are strong-willed and adventurous. It's a world influenced by the loss of Pullman's father at a young age, and by his family, whose world travels inspired the great adventures that he reimagines.

Pullman is an award-winning author widely recognized as a master of storytelling. He has written fairy tales, epic novels, detective stories, and fantasy. His works are critically acclaimed. He may be best known

Philip Pullman is the award-winning author of more than forty novels, short stories, and plays. He is most well known for the international best-selling trilogy *His Dark Materials*. His books have sold more than fifteen million copies and have been translated into forty different languages.

worldwide for his best-selling trilogy, *His Dark Materials*, an epic story inspired by literary greats John Milton, William Blake, and Heinrich von Kleist. It has been hailed as a modern fantasy classic and has been adapted into stage productions and films.

In the United Kingdom, Pullman's books are outsold only by J. K. Rowling's Harry Potter series. He has been compared to J. R. R. Tolkien, author of *The Hobbit* and *The Lord of the Rings* trilogy, and C. S. Lewis, author of *The Narnia Chronicles*—two of the greatest British fantasy authors of the twentieth century.

But Pullman is more than an author and more than the creator of new worlds and the captain of adventures. He began his career as a middle school teacher. Looking for a way to inspire his students, he used the last fifteen minutes of his class time to tell stories. Pullman turned some of these tales into school plays, and some even evolved into his first children's books.

His own world began to change when, in 1995, he published *Northern Lights* (retitled *The Golden Compass* in the United States), the first of three books in a trilogy that he titled *His Dark Materials*. Heavily influenced by Milton's *Paradise Lost*, Pullman's trilogy is a bold, adventurous retelling of the biblical Adam and Eve story. Among other things, it challenges people's perspectives on religion, which has generated a lot of controversy. The series became a best seller, and Pullman was hailed as both the "most significant" and the "most dangerous" writer in all of Great Britain.

Pullman has used his celebrity as a soapbox, engaging in debate over organized religion, the British education system, and the protection and championing of human rights.

ONE

CHAPTER

THE EARLY YEARS

Before Philip Pullman became a best-selling novelist, before his books were made into films, stage productions, and television movies, before he even realized he wanted to be a writer, he was a young boy who idolized his father and reveled in the adventures of comic book heroes and literary icons.

Pullman was born in Norwich, England, on October 19, 1946. His father, Alfred Outram Pullman, was a pilot for the Royal Air Force, a branch of the British armed forces. His father's job took the family to exotic places around the world. This included Southern Rhodesia (now known as Zimbabwe), a British colony in Southern Africa, where Pullman first attended school. When his father's tour of duty in Southern Africa came to an end, the family returned to the United Kingdom, where his father continued his military career.

Pullman's father was a pilot for the Royal Air Force. He flew a plane called the Harvard, which was a single-engine aircraft used at the time by the Royal Air Force, the U.S. Air Force, and the South African Air Force.

A FAMILY TRAGEDY AND A FATHER'S SECRETS

In 1953, when Pullman was seven years old, his mother received a telegram informing the family that his father had been killed in a plane crash while on a mission during the Mau Mau Uprising. This was a military conflict that took place in Kenya, a country in Southern Africa. Pullman's father led a squadron of planes during the conflict. Pullman had described his father as "a hero, steeped in glamour, killed in action defending his country." Shortly after his death, his father was awarded the Distinguished Flying Cross, an honor presented to the family by Queen Elizabeth II at Buckingham Palace.

Later in life, Pullman would learn two shocking facts about his father's death. First, that the Royal Air Force was bombing the lesser-armed Mau Mau, a tribal group that did not present much of a threat to the British armed forces. The Mau Mau did not have weapons they could use to defend themselves against military planes, but the Royal Air Force continued to conduct air assaults. Second, Pullman learned that his father had incurred large gambling debts. He was suspected of committing suicide by crashing his plane during the mission. Pullman later wrote about his father's death, saying to the English newspaper the *Independent*, "Sometimes I think he's really alive somewhere, in hiding, with a different name. I'd love to meet him."

Pullman describes this new information as "a serious challenge to his childhood memory" of his father. This memory of a heroic and perfect father would be tarnished further by the discovery of a third surprise: that his parents were in the midst of a divorce at the time of his father's death. Pullman learned of the end of his parent's relationship after his mother's death in 1989, when he found separation paperwork while he was settling her affairs.

DISCOVERING THE MAGIC AND MYSTERY OF STORYTELLING

Pullman's mother, Audrey Evelyn Pullman, was a homemaker. When her sons grew older, she eventually went to work for the British Broadcasting Corporation (BBC). She remarried after the death of her husband. Pullman and his younger brother, Francis, moved to Australia with their mother and new stepfather. Like their father, their stepfather was a Royal Air Force pilot.

Pullman, now nearly ten years old, was discovering novels and comic books for the first time. He loved reading and was especially drawn to Superman and Batman. In an essay he wrote for *Something About the Author Autobiography Series (SAAS)*, Pullman said, "When one day my stepfather brought me a Superman comic, it changed my life. I'd been a reader for a long time, but a reader of books; I'd never known comics. When I got this one, I devoured it and demanded more. I adored them."

He began collecting comic books as a hobby, a pastime he still enjoys today. He soon realized that these comics were a gateway to his own storytelling future. Pullman wrote in his *SAAS* essay, "What

I wanted was to *brood* over the world of Batman and dream actively. It was the first stirring of the storytelling impulse. I couldn't have put it like this, but what I wanted was to take characters, a setting, words, and pictures, and weave a pattern out of them; not *be* Batman, but write about him. I knew instinctively at once, that the telling of stories was delicious, and it all belonged to me."

Pullman, though newly enthralled by comic books, was also devouring books of all kinds. It almost didn't matter what the story was about Pullman found himself absorbed in other worlds, in mysteries, and in adventures. When he read Sir Arthur Conan Doyle's *The Adventures of Sherlock Holmes*, Pullman called the book "the most gripping, terrifying, thrilling story in the world."

It was around this time that he began to develop a talent for storytelling. He found comfort in creating parallel universes and enjoyed entertaining his brother late at night with ghost stories he would create. In an interview with Scholastic, in which Pullman Answered questions posed by his readers, he recalled:

I don't know whether he enjoyed it, or whether he even listened, but it wasn't for his benefit; it

Pullman found a new world to explore when he began reading comic books. He has said of comic books, "When one day my stepfather brought me a Superman comic, it changed my life." He also expressed a desire to enter the world of Batman and create his own adventures within it.

was for mine. I remember vividly the sense of diving into the dark as I began the story, with no idea at all what was going to happen or whether the story would "come out" as I called it, by which I meant make sense or come to a neat end. I remember the exhilaration of the risk: Would I find something to say? Would I dry

THE IMPORTANCE OF TRAVEL TO THE IMAGINATION

The family traveled frequently, and Philip Pullman counts these experiences, along with the death of his father, among those that have inspired his writing the most. At the time, the family traveled by ship, rather than airplane. "I'm very thankful that I lived at a time before universal air travel meant that I didn't have a chance to realize how big the world was." He added in a separate interview that "doing that, you come to see things that you just wouldn't notice when you fly. I mean, things like flying fishes and whales and the way the color of the ocean changes around the far south of Africa. And how the feeling of the ship changes with the different shape of the waves," he said in an interview with Scholastic. These physical memories have remained very real and vivid to Pullman. He has used some of them in his writing.

up? And I remember the thrill, the bliss, when, a minute ahead of getting there, I saw a twist I could give to the end, a clever way of bringing back that character who'd come into it earlier and vanished inconclusively, a neat phrase to tie it all up with. Many other things happened in Australia, but my discovery of storytelling was by far the most important.

RELIGION, READING, AND FREEDOM

Pullman and his brother were sent back to the United Kingdom, first to attend prep school and later a state school in Harlech, North West Wales. Pullman began spending more time with his grandfather, a Norfolk clergyman, who took him and his brother to church on Sundays and told the young boys stories from the Bible. In his *SAAS* essay, Pullman noted that his grandfather was "the center of the world. There was no one stronger than he was, or wiser, or kinder... When I was young, he was the sun at the center of my life." His grandfather was a gifted storyteller. "He took the simplest little event and made a story out of it," Pullman wrote.

By the time Pullman was fifteen years old, he was writing poetry. Fueling his imagination were two things:

An illustration by Gustave Doré that dramatizes the fall of man, as depicted in John Milton's epic poem *Paradise Lost*. Pullman cites *Paradise Lost* as one of the main inspirations behind his trilogy, *His Dark Materials*.

the vast collection of books he read and the freedom he had to play. His closest friend lived a couple of miles away, and Pullman thought nothing of wandering through the woods to go visit him. It's these freedoms and the sense of creativity they can bring, he said to the English newspaper the *Telegraph*, that children don't get to enjoy anymore. "Children don't have to go and entertain themselves any more as we did, and I am sure that we benefited from it. They seem to have less chance to experience the things like being bored, or darkness, real darkness, and silence. I am sure that my imagination was strengthened and fed by the things I had to do in order to play.'"

It was around this time that Pullman discovered John Milton's *Paradise Lost*, an epic poem published in 1667 that centers around two stories. One features Satan; the other, Adam and Eve. The poem is a reimagining of the biblical story of Adam and Eve. *Paradise Lost* would later inspire Pullman's writing and become a significant influence upon the *His Dark Materials* trilogy.

TEACHING AND WRITING

After graduating from prep school, Pullman attended Exeter College, Oxford, where he studied English. He told Scholastic, "My favorite subject was English, partly because it was all about reading, and I loved reading books. Spelling and grammar and that kind of thing came very easily to me, unlike science and mathematics, which I found much harder."

Pullman married his wife, Judith Speller, a teacher, in 1970. They have two sons, Jamie, a professional viola player, and Tom, a linguist. Pullman's first published work, a novel titled *The Haunted Storm*, came out in 1972. He was only twenty-five at the time. While the book was well received by literary critics—it was a co-winner of the New English Library's Young Writer's Award—Pullman is dismissive of the project. He says now that he wrote the book out of a sense of duty, rather than conviction.

Even though he was now a published author, his book was not successful enough to financially support his family and enable him to write full-time. So he took a job at Moss Bros. in Covent Garden, selling men's clothing. After a year and a half, Pullman found a job as a librarian before being trained as a teacher. He published one novel during this time, an adult fantasy-fiction work called *Galatea* (1976).

For the next twelve years, Pullman taught Greek mythology and English at two different middle schools in Oxford. He found that orally recounting the exploits of the Greek gods and heroes in Homer's *The Iliad* and *The Odyssey* was helping hone his own abilities as a powerful storyteller. As he said in his *SAAS* essay,

*[The] real beneficiary of all that storytelling
wasn't so much the audience as the storyteller. I'd chosen—for what I thought, and
think still, were good educational reasons—to
do something that, by a lucky chance, was the
best possible training for me as a writer. To tell
great stories over and over again, testing and
refining the language and observing the reac-
tion of the listeners and gradually improving
the timing and the rhythm and the pace, was
to undergo an apprenticeship that probably
wasn't very different, essentially, from the one
that Homer himself underwent three thousand
years ago.*

While Pullman describes his teaching skills as
"variable" or fickle, former students rave about
his ability to teach and inspire. Greta Stoddart, an
award-winning poet, was a student of Pullman's
when she attended Bishop Kirk Middle School.
Stoddart says of Pullman in the *Telegraph*, "He had
an extraordinary energy. And he didn't need books.
He would come in and just launch into some story.
All of us girls were a bit in love with him."

It was while teaching that Pullman began writing plays for his students to perform. He told the
Telegraph in an interview, "The first one I did was

Philip Pullman partners with the London Zoo to launch Find Your Daemon, an interactive exhibit based on the *His Dark Materials* trilogy. The exhibit helps participants find their own daemon, or animal spirit, among the animals at the zoo.

called *Spring-Heeled Jack*, and it was a sort of melodrama, with an outrageous villain and larger-than-life heroes and comic policeman and that sort of thing." He found joy in writing the plays and seeing where his active imagination could take him. He wrote more than six different plays, each performed at the end of the year by his students. These early works inspired Pullman to begin writing children's books, which led him to become one of the most gifted authors of children's literature in the last fifty years.

BECOMING A NOVELIST

Philip Pullman enjoyed writing school plays so much that he soon turned to writing children's books. His first book for young readers was *Count Karlstein* (1982), the plot of which originated in one of his school plays.

The story, set in 1816 in the fictional Swiss village of Karlstein, tells the story of how Count Karlstein made a deal with a demon huntsman named Zamiel to become vastly wealthy. A condition of the deal was that in ten years, on All Soul's Eve, the count must present a human sacrifice of his choosing to Zamiel. He choses his two young nieces, setting in motion a cast of characters—the castle maid, a coachman, the girls' teacher, and the count's lawyer— who all work to save the girls.

Pullman, at the British Library in London, is awarded the Astrid Lindgren Memorial Award for Children's and Youth Literature. The honor is awarded by the Swedish government and is the second largest literature prize in the world.

SALLY LOCKHART

Pullman found that he enjoyed writing for a younger audience. In 1985, he published *The Ruby in the Smoke*, a historical novel that became the first of a series of books featuring Sally Lockhart, a smart, savvy, sixteen-year-old teenager. Lockhart gets involved in the opium trade when she receives a cryptic note soon after her father drowns off the coast of Singapore.

The book was popular with both readers and critics. Peter Hollindale, of the *British Book News Children's Books*, wrote, "This is a splendid book… It is a first-rate adventure story." Brooke L. Dillon wrote in the *Voice of Youth Advocates*, "Pullman respects his teenaged audience enough to treat them to a complex, interwoven plot." Pullman himself said that he first found his voice as a children's author when writing this novel.

The second book in the series, *The Shadow in the Plate*, was published in the United Kingdom in 1986 (the book was renamed *The Shadow in the North* when it was published in the United States). Lockhart is now a young woman who

llowing years of being a middle school teacher, Pullman took a job as a senior cturer at Westminster College *(above)*, where he taught writing to college-age udents. While teaching at the college, Pullman wrote the last two novels in the lly Lockhart series.

works as a financial consultant. She joins forces with Frederick Garland, a photographer-turned-detective who was first introduced to readers in *The Ruby in the Smoke.* They work together to solve a mystery that involves the aristocracy, the Spiritualism movement, and a conspiracy centered on the production of a weapon. The book was a hit with critics. Michael Cart, of *School Library Journal*, wrote that Pullman "once again demon-strates his mastery of atmosphere and style."

In 1987, Pullman left his job as a middle school teacher to take a position as a senior lecturer at Westminster College. Even though he was now teaching writing to college students, he continued to publish additional books featuring the teen-aged Sally Lockhart. Two more Lockhart novels followed. The third, *The Tiger in the Well* (1990), finds Lockhart as a successful tycoon who is also a single mother with a two-year-old daughter named Harriet. In the final Lockhart book, *The Tin Princess* (1994), the little girl who disappears at the end of *The Ruby in the Smoke* turns up again in a surprising place. Lockhart makes only a short appearance in this novel as two new heroines, Adelaide and Becky, get caught up in the intrigue and mystery.

By the late 1990s, Pullman had published a steady stream of children's books, including *How* to Be Cool (1987), *The Broken Bridge* (1990), *The White Mercedes* (1992), and *The Firework-Maker's Daughter* (1995). Now an accomplished and successful writer, Pullman decided to quit teaching to write full-time.

PULLMAN'S APPROACH TO WRITING

Like many writers, Pullman has a special place where he retreats to write his novels and allow his creativity to flow freely. Initially, that place was a small shed located in the garden on his property. He began writing in the shed when his oldest son started taking violin lessons. Pullman needed a quiet place away from where his son was practicing. It became the place where he was best able to tap into and draw out his creativity. When he returned from a long day of teaching, his "real life began" out in the shed, he has said.

Pullman has a unique writing style. He limits himself to writing only three pages per day, by hand, using pen and paper. In an interview with RodCorp that details how he works, Pullman said, "I write three pages every day (one side of the paper only). That's about 1,100 words. Then I stop, having made sure to write the first sentence on the next page so I never have a blank page facing me in the morning."

PULLMAN'S FAMOUS SHED

Cobwebs, an old computer, masks, a 6-foot [1.8-meter] fluffy rat, posters, and children's drawings: this assortment of odds and ends provided the décor inside Philip Pullman's shed. The shed was located in a small corner of his garden, and Pullman retreated to this tiny, cluttered space to write his novels. Over the years, through his research and other endeavors, he had accumulated these interesting little pieces of life. The crowded space had never been cleaned, partly because Pullman was superstitious about moving anything, fearful that he would disrupt his creativity and alter his ability to write.

But when celebrity took over and fans began stopping by his house, Pullman and his wife decided it was time to move on. After they moved to a larger home, he faced a decision about whether to take the shed with him. Instead of moving the shed, he decided to leave it behind for another artist, an illustrator named Ted Dewan. But there was one condition: Dewan must pass the shed along to another artist when he was through with it.

In the years since Pullman left it behind, the shed has become a place for other writers to hone their craft. In an interview with RodCorp, Pullman once said of his decision to leave the shed to a succession of other artists, "I like the idea that it'll get passed on to lots of other writers and illustrators, and each of them will replace this bit or that bit until there isn't an atom of the original shed left."

Once a story is finished, Pullman types it out on a computer, editing as he transcribes his book. "Then I read it all again and think it's horrible and get very depressed," he said. "That's one of the things you have to put up with. Eventually, after a lot of fiddling, it's sort of all right, but the best I can do; and that's when I send it off to the publisher."

Pullman has a daily writing routine. When he's working on a book, he gets up in the morning, has tea and breakfast with his wife, then goes into his study to write until lunchtime. He takes a break for lunch and watches *Neighbours*, an Australian soap opera. When the show is over, he takes his two dogs, pugs named Hoagy and Nellie, for a walk. He then either returns to writing if he hasn't yet finished his three pages, or he works on non-writing projects. Pullman likes routine, as he told the *Telegraph*: "I have never been interested in travelling really. It's uncomfortable, hot, full of foreigners. I don't like going away. I am an old misery. I like staying at home."

THE NEW CUT GANG

In the mid-1990s, as he was completing the Sally Lockhart novels, Pullman began writing a new set of books. They were set in the 1890s in Lambeth, a neighborhood in central London. The books featured a group of poor, young, scrappy detectives who ranged in age from six to thirteen. The first book, *Thunderbolt's Waxwork*, was published in 1994, the second, *The Gasfitter's Ball*, in 1995. Pullman said of the setting for the books, "I realized that London at that time was very rich in different communities mixing and getting on with each other: Jewish, Irish, Italian, and I thought, 'Ooh, that's fun.' It gives an interest to the background and helps with the language" (as quoted in the *Telegraph*).

The books starred Jewish genius Benny Kaminsky, feisty Irish Bridie, brainy-but-clumsy Sam "Thunderbolt" Dobney, and the devilish Italian Peretti twins. These adventurous kids find allies in eccentric

Pullman's New Cut Gang novels are set in the 1890s in Lambeth, a neighborhood in London. This is an illustration of Lambeth Palace and the Thames River in London created by Reverend Richard Lovett.

characters who help them fight against thieves, bookies, pickpockets, and counterfeiters on the streets of London.

Critics love the two novels. the *Sunday Times* said the *New Cut Gang* books are "fast, funny, gripping stuff." In reviewing the novels, the *Observer* called Pullman "an extraordinary writer." Pullman planned to expand the series, adding four to five new titles. But as fate would have it, a new series, born from a chance conversation, would steer him in a different direction and launch his career internationally.

A BEST-SELLING SERIES IS BORN

For years, Philip Pullman was a respected author of children's books, churning out solid works that gained him critical acclaim and a growing legion of fans. He had a solid following of readers who eagerly awaited his newest releases. But all of that changed in 1995, when he published *Northern Lights*. When the first book in the *His Dark Materials* trilogy launched, Pullman became an international best-selling author.

A CHANCE CONVERSATION

As Pullman plotted out the next stories of the New Cut Gang, the editor who had commissioned the series left the publishing house. The editors who took over had little interest in new installments for the series. Pullman's publisher, David Fickling, took him to lunch one afternoon and, as Pullman

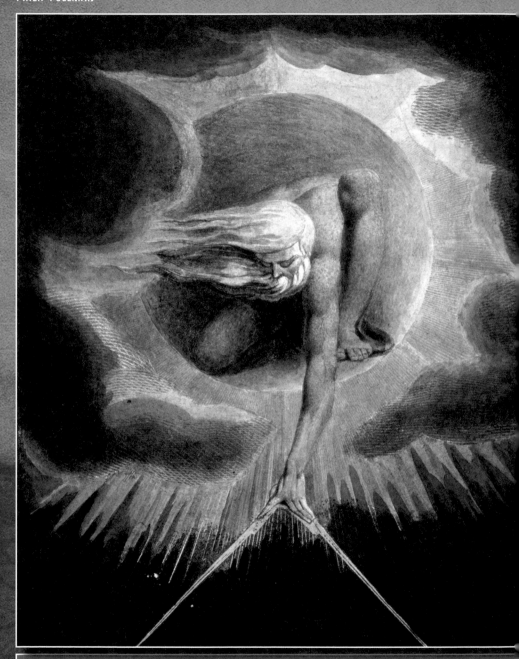

This watercolor is titled *The Ancient of Days*, by William Blake. Blake's works served as an inspiration to Pullman as he wrote *His Dark Materials*. Blake's *America: A Prophecy* and its sequel, *Europe: A Prophecy*, both deal with upheavals that are traced back to the misunderstanding of Christianity.

describes the conversation in an interview with the *Telegraph*, "We somehow got onto Milton's *Paradise Lost*, which we had both studied [in school] and both loved. We sat quoting large chunks to each other, and, by the end of the meal, I had somehow agreed to write a fantasy...not based on *Paradise Lost* but with the same sort of atmosphere."

Pullman says of the initial conversation with Fickling: "Off the top of my head I improvised a kind of fantasia on themes from Book 2 of *Paradise Lost*. And [Fickling] got quite excited because he loves *Paradise Lost* as well. By this time, I knew the kind of thing I wanted to do—I knew the length, I knew it was going to be in three volumes, and I knew it was going to be big and ambitious and enable me to say things I'd never been able to say in any other form."

But truth be told, Pullman had been thinking about writing a book loosely based on *Paradise Lost* for quite some time. For several years, he had been collecting different pieces of litera-ture that he found interesting or that served as touchstones or inspirations that were leading him toward the concept for *His Dark Materials*. Among the literary figures that inspired him were English poet and printmaker William Blake and the German novelist Heinrich von Kleist.

Pullman began writing the first book, *Northern Lights*, which was retitled *The Golden Compass* in the United States. He found a number of his ideas starting to come together as he created his main character, Lyra Belacqua, a twelve-year-old orphaned tomboy. He also soon realized that *Paradise Lost* was a larger inspiration for his new series even than he had first believed. But he also knew that he was also just reworking fertile ground that was fundamental to the human experience, human understanding, and artistic effort. He told the *Economist's* MoreIntelligenLife.com, "I didn't think on the one hand, 'Oh, bugger, I'm telling the same story,' or, on the other hand, 'Oh great, I can copy it.' I just realized that, in his patch, Milton had been working on the same thing. And, a long time ago, the original writer of the book of Genesis had been working on the same story."

Northern Lights was published in 1995 and was an immediate success. The *Guardian* described it as "an eye-widening fantasy, a scorching thriller, and a thought-provoking reflection on the human condition."

NORTHERN LIGHTS

Northern Lights, the first book in the *His Dark Materials* trilogy, introduces to readers Pullman's heroine, Lyra Belacqua. She is a young girl who lives in a world where humans are always accompanied by daemons, or animals who embody the souls of their humans. Lyra and her daemon, Pantalaimon, have been raised in the isolated world of Jordan College.

Lyra accidently learns about the existence of Dust, a strange particle discovered by her uncle, Lord Asriel. A powerful Church organization, called the Magisterium, believes Dust to be related to Original Sin. Scientific research has proven that Dust is less attracted to children than to adults. To learn why this is, and to prevent children from acquiring Dust when they are older, children are kidnapped by the Magisterium. Experiments are then conducted to separate these children from their daemons.

A woman named Mrs. Coulter has been directing these experiments in the North with scientists from the Magisterium. The Master of Jordan College, who has been raising Lyra, turns her over to Mrs. Coulter under pressure from the Church. But he first gives Lyra an alethiometer, an instrument that can reveal any truth or answer any question when properly used. The alethiometer uses Dust to produce its knowledge. Lyra soon discovers that Mrs. Coulter, an elegant and beautiful woman, is the head of the General Oblation Board, the group that is rumored to be the ones behind the child kidnappings and experiments with Dust.

Actress Dakota Blue Richards stars as Lyra Belacqua in *The Golden Compass*, the first and only book in the *His Dark Materials* trilogy to be made into a film.

Scared, Lyra runs away. Gyptians, who live on riverboats, rescue her. She learns from them that Mrs. Coulter is actually her mother and that Lord Asriel is her father, not her uncle. Lyra goes with the Gyptians on an expedition to rescue the missing children and to look for her best friend, Roger Parslow, who she believes was kidnapped. Aided by a clan of witches, Lyra and the Gyptians save the children and find Roger.

Lyra believes that she is supposed to bring her alethiometer to Lord Asriel, only to learn that she is instead destined to bring him a child, who ends up being Roger. Lord Asriel has been working to build a bridge to another world, a world that can only be seen in the sky through the northern lights. The bridge requires a vast amount of energy to open the boundary between the two worlds. Asriel severs Roger from his daemon, killing Roger in the process and giving himself the energy he needs to gain access to the new world. Asriel enters the new world. Lyra and Pantalaimon follow him.

THE SUBTLE KNIFE

In 1997, the second book in the trilogy, *The Subtle Knife*, was published. In this continuation of *The Northern Lights*, Lyra finds herself in Cittàgazze, a city in the new world on the other side of the bridge. The citizens of Cittàgazze have been reckless in their use of technology, which has released Spectres, or soul eaters. Children are immune to these Spectres, who render much of the new world inaccessible to adults.

Lyra meets Will Parry, a twelve-year-old boy from her world. Will has just killed a man to protect his sick mother. He then stumbled upon Cittàgazze, where he is searching for his long-lost father. Will becomes the bearer of the Subtle Knife, a tool

THE BEST-SELLING *HIS DARK MATERIALS* SERIES

Philip Pullman's *His Dark Materials* trilogy has been translated into forty languages and has sold more than fifteen million copies worldwide. In his home country of Great Britain, only one author outsells his books: J. K. Rowling, whose Harry Potter series is also a worldwide sensation.

Pullman's books are critically acclaimed. The trilogy, along with its author, has been recognized with a number of honors:

- *Northern Lights* won the Carnegie Medal for children's fiction in the United Kingdom in 1995.
- The *Observer* cites *Northern Lights* as one of the one hundred best novels.
- The *His Dark Materials* trilogy came in third place in the 2003 BBC's Big Read, a national poll of viewers' favorite books (behind *The Lord of the Rings* and *Pride and Prejudice*).
- In 2001, *The Amber Spyglass* won the prestigious Whitbread Book of the Year award, the first time the award was given to a children's book.
- In May 2005, Pullman received the Swedish government's Astrid Lindgren Memorial Award for children's and youth literature.
- *The Amber Spyglass* won the *Guardian* Children's Book Award.

forged three hundred years ago. One edge of the sword can divide subatomic particles and create portals between worlds. The other edge can easily cut through any form of matter. Aided by witches, Lyra and Will find Will's father, who is murdered before them by a witch who loves him but whom he has rejected. Lyra is then kidnapped by her mother, Mrs. Coulter.

THE AMBER SPYGLASS

The Amber Spyglass, the third novel in the series, was published in 2000. In this final chapter of the saga, Mrs. Coulter learns of the prophecy that Lyra

Northern Lights is the original title of the first book in Pullman's *His Dark Materials* trilogy. When the book was released in the United States, its name was changed to *The Golden Compass*.

has been identified as the next Eve. Mrs. Coulter hides Lyra in a remote cave to protect her from the Magisterium, who want to kill her.

A pair of angels, Balthamos and Baruch, informs Will Parry that he must travel with them to give the Subtle Knife to Lyra's father, Lord Asriel, who will use it against the Authority—the first angel to come into existence and the one who created Dust. Will ignores the angels and instead teams with spies, a local girl named Ama, and the Bear King to rescue Lyra.

With Lyra, the group travels to the Land of the Dead. They join forces with Mary Malone, a scientist from Will's home world, who has been researching Dust. She learns that the true nature of Dust is self-awareness. Lord Asriel and Mrs. Coulter destroy the Authority but die in the process. When Will and Lyra emerge from the Land of the Dead, they fall in love but soon realize they cannot live together in the same world because all windows into the different worlds must be closed to prevent the loss of Dust. They also learn that each of them can only live a full life upon return to his or her own native world. Will and Lyra decide to part ways. Lyra loses her ability to read the alethiometer and decides that she will instead learn how to use her conscious mind to achieve divination.

The Amber Spyglass is the third and final novel in the *His Dark Materials* series. It was published in 2000 and concludes Lyra's journey. The book won the *Guardian* Children's Book Award.

COMPANION BOOKS
DEEPEN LYRA'S WORLD

Pullman decided that the end of *His Dark Materials* trilogy, which concluded with *The Amber Spyglass*, wasn't really the final word on Lyra's story. In 2003,

Pullman and his wife, Jude, celebrate after *The Amber Spyglass* is awarded the prestigious Whitbread Book of the Year Award. It is the first time a children's book has ever won the award.

he published *Lyra's Oxford*, a companion book that serves as a stepping-stone beyond the trilogy. *Lyra's Oxford* takes place a few years after *The Amber Spyglass.* Lyra is older and more mature. She attends a school for girls at Oxford. The book includes artifacts that help readers connect with Lyra and her world at Oxford. These include a map, a postcard from Dr. Mary Malone, and a cruise brochure. The text makes reference to characters from the first three books, including Will Parry, who now serves as a source of inspiration for Lyra, rather than a lost love, as he was when the trilogy ended.

Pullman is currently developing a concept for another book, possibly a two-volume set, tentatively titled *The Book of Dust*. In an interview with the *Telegraph*, Pullman revealed some early information about his plans: "I think it might be in two volumes, and I think one might take place in the time before *His Dark Materials*, and the other might take place afterwards." The volumes will not be a continuation of Lyra's story, but rather it will address questions that have been raised about Pullman's negative treatment of organized religion in *His Dark Materials.* And while it will take place in the same world as the earlier books, it will focus its attention on other characters besides Lyra and Will and on new story lines.

HIS DARK MATERIALS CAST OF CHARACTERS

Lyra Belacqua—A young girl who inhabits a universe parallel to our own. She is the daughter of Lord Asriel and Marisa Coulter.

Will Parry—The son of John Parry, an explorer. He becomes friends with and falls in love with Lyra Belacqua. He also becomes the bearer of the Subtle Knife.

Lord Asriel—A member of the English aristocracy and the father of Lyra Belacqua.

Mrs. Coulter—The head of the General Oblation Board and the director of experiments on kidnapped children. She is also the mother of Lyra Belacqua.

Iorek Byrnison—The king of the armored bears in his homeland, Svalbard. He follows a strict code of conduct in which he will not, under any circumstances, break a promise that he has made.

John Faa—Also known as Lord Faa, the Lord of the Western Gyptians, who ends up saving children kidnapped by Mrs. Coulter.

Farder Coram—The second-in-command and adviser to the Gyptian King, Lord Faa.

Serafina Pekkala—The witch queen of Inari, Finland; accompanies Lyra Belacqua on her journey.

Lee Scoresby—An aeronaut balloonist who pledges his support to Lord Faa and the Gyptians as they set out on their mission to save the kidnapped children.

John Parry—The father of Will Parry and a famous English explorer who goes missing. It's his son, Will, who goes in search of his father.

Iofur Raknison—An armor-wearing, intelligent polar bear.

The Authority—The first angel to come into existence. He also formed the substance known as Dust.

Balthamos and Baruch—Same-sex partners who are angels in rebellion against the Kingdom of Heaven. They want to become part of Lord Asriel's army.

Dr. Mary Malone—A physicist from Will's world who is researching Dust. She is the one who eventually learns the purpose of Dust.

Chevalier Tialys—Serves as a spy to Lord Asriel.

Lady Salmakia—With her partner Chevalier Tialys, she is sent to guide Lyra Belacqua and Will Parry on their journey.

Roger Parslow—The best friend of Lyra Belacqua during her early life in Jordan College.

Metatron—The true antagonist of the trilogy; he seeks to supplant the Authority, destroy Lord Asriel and his army, and kill the heroine Lyra Belacqua.

On his Web site, Pullman also addresses the question of whether he will return to writing additional novels starring Sally Lockhart, or at the very least, set in her world. While he is currently working on *The Book of Dust*, he does plan to return to Sally Lockhart once he has the time.

SUCCESS AND CONTROVERSY

When Philip Pullman published the first of the three books in the *His Dark Materials* trilogy, he became an international sensation. Readers around the world fell in love with Lyra Belacqua, Will Parry, and their amazing journey into new worlds. Fans waited impatiently for the next two books in the series to be released.

With the winning of that many fans, one also earns a few detractors. Because God is killed in the course of the stories, Pullman has been called the "most significant" and "most dangerous" writer in all of Great Britain. Even so, the *His Dark Materials* trilogy has garnered international success. The books have been translated into forty languages and have sold more than fifteen million copies worldwide.

STAGE AND FILM ADAPTATIONS

The *His Dark Materials* series spawned a stage production in 2003 and 2004 at the Royal National Theatre in London. The three sprawling novels were condensed into two three-hour plays. The production begins with Lyra Belacqua and Will Parry meeting on a park bench while still existing within their different worlds. From there, the plays serve as a retrospective guide to the journey that they take throughout the trilogy. A new version of the stage production was completed in 2009 and toured much of the United Kingdom during its four-month run.

In addition to a stage production, *Northern Lights* (retitled *The Golden Compass* in the United States) was optioned as a film. Starring Academy Award–winning actress Nicole Kidman as Mrs. Coulter and Daniel Craig as Lord Asriel, the movie was released in theaters in December 2007. The cast included both American and British actors, including well-known performers such as Kathy Bates, Kristin Scott Thomas, Ian McShane, Ian McKellan, Freddie Highmore, and newcomer Dakota Blue Richards as Lyra Belacqua. The film had a $180 million production budget. In the United States, it earned $70 million. In the United Kingdom, the film grossed more than $53 million and became the second-highest-grossing film (that was not a sequel) in 2007.

The *His Dark Materials* trilogy was adapted as a stage production at the Royal National Theatre. The play, a two-part, six-hour performance, was a huge success and was revived just one year later. The production has since appeared in Dublin, Ireland, and theaters throughout England.

The film drew fair reviews. James Christopher of the *Times* was disappointed in the production. While he praised the special effects, calling them "marvelous," he said of the overall film that the "books weave a magic the film simply cannot match." Famous movie critic Roger Ebert gave the film four out of four stars, saying it was "a darker, deeper fantasy epic than *The Chronicles of Narnia* or the [*Harry*] *Potter* films." He also added that the film "creates villains that are more complex and poses more intriguing questions. As a visual experience, it is superb." The film won several awards, among them the 2008 BAFTA (British Academy of Film and Television Arts) for Special Visual Effects and an Academy Award for Best Visual Effects.

While screenplays were being developed for two sequels, based on *The Subtle Knife* and *The Amber Spyglass*, both projects were put on hold indefinitely when *The Golden Compass* did not meet box office revenue expectations in the United States. Though *The Golden Compass* performed much better internationally, the film studio decided against producing the next two installments.

In 2009, Pullman's novel *The White Mercedes* was made into a film. Retitled *The Butterfly Tattoo*, it centers on a young man named Chris and a girl named Jenny. The two fall in love, while things that happened in their pasts begin to catch up with them. The film won a number of awards at film festivals around the world. These awards included Best Adaptation and Best Director at the New York International Independent Film and Video Festival, Best Feature Film at the Columbus (Ohio) International Film and Video Festival, and Best Film at the Beaufort (South Carolina) International Film Festival. While it was a small production, the film has attracted considerable attention on the Internet. It has been illegally downloaded more than two hundred thousand times.

The film version of *The Golden Compass* was the second-highest-grossing film (that was not a sequel) in 2007 in the United Kingdom. It went on to win several awards, including a 2008 BAFTA (British Academy of Film and Television Arts) for Special Visual Effects and an Academy Award for Best Visual Effects.

The BBC also made *His Dark Materials* into a radio drama. It was broadcast in 2003 and is now available on CD.

AN AWARD-WINNING AUTHOR

In addition to the Carnegie Medal, the *Guardian* Children's Fiction Prize, the Astrid Lindgren Memorial Award, and the Whitbread Book of the Year award, Pullman was on the short list of authors nominated for the 2011 Man Booker International Prize. This award recognizes one outstanding living author every two years for his or her achievement in fiction. In 2001, Pullman's *The Amber Spyglass* was long-listed for the Man

Among the multiple adaptations of *His Dark Materials* is a radio drama and multiple stage productions, including one at the Playhouse Theatre in Oxford, England. Pullman poses with puppets that appear in the Playhouse production.

Booker Prize, which promotes the finest fiction by honoring the best book of the year.

His Dark Materials wasn't the only work of Pullman's to be recognized. In 1995, Pullman won the Nestle Smarties award, one of the most respected and prestigious prizes for children's literature. The award was given for his children's novels *Clockwork* and *The Firework-Maker's Daughter.*

In 2007, Pullman was made an honorary professor at Bangor University in North Wales. In 2008, he returned to his teaching roots when he became a Fellow in the Master of Arts program in creative writing at Oxford Brookes University, in Oxford, England. Later that year, he hosted "The Writer's Table" for Waterstone's, a British bookstore chain that has more than 288 stores throughout the United Kingdom and Europe. At the Waterstone's event, Pullman gave a presentation in which he highlighted the forty books that have most influenced his career.

In October 2009, Pullman became a patron of the Palestine Festival of Literature, an annual arts event in the Middle East. He is also a patron of the Shakespeare Schools Festival, the United Kingdom's largest youth drama festival. The festival targets underprivileged schoolchildren and their teachers and enables them to perform Shakespeare at local professional theaters all over the United Kingdom.

THE WAY WE UNDERSTAND STORIES

Philip Pullman, while speaking at the University of East Anglia in Norwich, England, at its annual lecture on religion and education, said how stories can teach us lessons in a way that religion cannot. He said, "I don't profess any religion; I don't think it's possible that there is a God; I have the greatest difficulty in understanding what is meant by the words 'spiritual' or 'spirituality'; but I think I can say something about moral education, and I think it has something to do with the way we understand stories."

What Pullman means is that stories have a way of reaching us and educating us with lasting visions of humanity. He told the audience, "We learn from Macbeth's fate that killing is horrible for the killer as well as the victim." He later said in an interview, "'Thou shalt not' might reach the head, but it takes 'Once upon a time' to reach the heart" (as quoted in the *New Yorker*).

Many fans and critics have asked Pullman to reveal what he means in his books, but he has so far refused, saying, "As a passionate believer in the democracy of reading, I don't think it's the task of the author of a book to tell the reader what it means. The meaning of a story emerges in the meeting between the words on the page and the thoughts in the reader's mind. So when people ask me what I meant by this story, or what was the message I was trying to convey in that one, I have to explain that I'm not going to explain. Anyway, I'm not in the message business; I'm in the 'Once upon a time' business" (as quoted in the *New Yorker*).

THE MOST DANGEROUS AUTHOR IN BRITAIN

Pullman is open about being an atheist—someone who does not believe in the presence of deities or gods proposed by organized religions. He said in an interview that he is "caught between the words 'atheist' and 'agnostic.' I've got no evidence whatever for believing in a God. But I know that all the things I do know are very small compared with the things that I don't know. So maybe there is a God out there. All I know if that is there is, he hasn't shown himself on earth."

Having being raised in a religious environment, with a grandfather who was a clergyman and always brought his grandson to church with him on Sundays, the exact source of Pullman's lack of belief in God and religion is unclear. But it has influenced his writing and drawn much criticism. Pullman's comments about organized religion, specifically Catholicism, have caused a lot of controversy. He has even received death threats. Many religious groups have taken offense at how Pullman has portrayed the Church, God, and religion in *His Dark Materials*. Some British newspapers, including the *Mail on Sunday*, have even gone so far as to describe Pullman as "the most

Pullman has been called the most dangerous author in Britain for his atheist beliefs. Pullman says he does not believe in God, but religion is present in most of his works.

dangerous author in Britain." The American-based Catholic League called for a boycott of *The Golden Compass* film, saying it "sells atheism to kids."

In an interview with the *Economist's* MoreIntelligentLife.com, Pullman asks people who take offense to read his books so that they can learn firsthand what he is writing about. He says if these critics did, "they'll find a story that attacks such things as cruelty, oppression, intolerance, unkindness, narrow-mindedness, and celebrates love, kindness, open-mindedness, tolerance, curiosity, human intelligence. It's very hard to disagree with those. But people will."

In general, Pullman does not address his critics head-on, preferring to focus on the stories he has written. He has made the occasional exception, once in a while discussing how controversy has fueled his books sales. Of Peter Hitchens, who called him "the most dangerous author in Britain," he said, "It's a great compliment to me, isn't it?" He framed Hitchens's article and posted it on his wall. Knowing controversy is good for book sales, Pullman later said, "Of course, I sent him a card of appreciation and thanks."

In an interview with NBC News, Pullman said of the content found within *His Dark Materials* and the intent behind its creation: "What I was mainly doing, I hope, was telling a story… As for the atheism, it doesn't matter to me whether people believe in God or not, so I'm not promoting anything of that sort. What I do care about is whether people are cruel or whether they're kind, whether they act for democracy or for tyranny, whether they believe in open-minded enquiry or in shutting the freedom of thought and expression. Good things have been done in the name of religion, and so have bad things; and both good things and bad things have been done with no religion at all. What I care about is the good, wherever it comes from."

THE GOOD MAN JESUS AND THE SCOUNDREL CHRIST

While Pullman may not take on his many critics directly, their comments and points of view have had little influence in preventing him from continuing to tackle the topic of religion in his writing. *The Good Man Jesus and the Scoundrel Christ*, published in 2010, is a work of fiction that challenges the events of the New Testament's four Gospels.

Pullman's book offers his own version of the life of Jesus. With that retelling have come heated debates and a frenzy of controversy throughout the religious and literary worlds. His is a bold retelling of the life of Jesus Christ. It suggests there were twin children born to Joseph and the Virgin Mary, the prophet Jesus and his trouble-making brother, Christ.

In the English newspaper the *Guardian*, Pullman says of the book, "I've always been fascinated by the difference between the man Jesus, the son of Joseph and Mary, who I think almost certainly existed, and the idea of Christ, the son of God. The vast bulk of what people say about Christ seems to me nonsense, impossible, absurd. About Jesus, on the other hand, we can say many interesting things."

JUGGLING FAIRY TALES AND ACTIVISM

While best known for the *His Dark Materials* trilogy, Philip Pullman has written a wide range of children's books and has even entered the adult fiction landscape with his critically acclaimed novel *The Good Man Jesus and the Scoundrel Christ*. The audience for his books is a mix of children and adults who find his works to be compelling and exciting.

Pullman has taken on several new projects in the years since *His Dark Materials* was published. He has had a chance to retell the Grimm fairy tales, and he's become an activist and humanitarian. He has evolved into an outspoken social warrior, a real-life counterpart to his fictional heroes, looking to right the wrongs committed in society against its most vulnerable members.

PULLMAN TAKES ON FAIRY TALES

Penguin Publishers approached Pullman about a special project: retelling Grimm's fairy tales for the bicentennial, or two hundredth anniversary, of the collection. The stories are a collection of German folk and fairy tales first published in 1812 by the Grimm brothers, Jacob and Wilhelm. These tales include "Cinderella," "Rapunzel," "Hansel and Gretel," "Snow White," "Rumpelstiltskin," and the "Golden Goose."

Penguin Classics, which had published a selection of Grimm's fairy tales thirty years ago, wanted Pullman to translate and author a new selection, a revised, more modern retelling of Grimm. Penguin gave him a complete collection of Grimm fairy tales from which to choose. In the newspaper the *Guardian*, Pullman says of the project, "I thought there were a couple of problems with the selected Grimm that they'd got, and that I could do it better. So I've spent much of the last year reading all

The seven dwarfs find Snow White asleep in their bedroom. This fairy tale, by the Brothers Grimm, is among the fifty Pullman chose as part of an annotated new collection of the Grimm Brothers' work.

the Grimm, choosing fifty of the tales, and writing them in my voice and annotating them."

The new collection, *Fairy Tales from the Brothers Grimm*, is a retelling of fifty stories selected by Pullman from the *Children's and Household Tales*, the original book of tales collected and told by the Grimm bothers. He was intrigued by the idea of returning to the stories he grew up hearing, as he told *Mother Jones* magazine:

> *I wanted the chance to look again at these very famous stories and see what made them work well, whether there were any ways in which they could be improved. Because the great thing about fairy tales and folk tales is that there is no authentic text. It's not like the text of* Paradise Lost *or* James Joyce's Ulysses, *and you have to adhere to that exact text. I thought there were things maybe I could play around with.*

Pullman's book includes many well-known fairy tales, such as "Little Red Riding Hood," "Cinderella," and "The Twelve Brothers." It also features many lesser-known tales, such as "The Three Snake Leaves," "The Brave Little Tailor," and "The Robber Bridegroom."

Jacob and Wilhelm Grimm, otherwise known as the Grimm Brothers, were German academics and authors who published large collections of fairy tales and folklore. Some of their most famous stories are "Cinderella," "Rapunzel," and "Snow White."

He was given creative freedom to choose which of the more than four hundred tales he wanted to rewrite. The *New York Times* wrote favorably about Pullman's task of taking on Grimm's fairy tales, saying, "Mr. Pullman keeps his touch light, lending the stories a plain-spoken, casual voice and respecting the strange trans-formations, reversals of fortune, and patterns of three that give them their power." Pullman himself says of the project, in an interview with Bookwitch:

> *One of the things I wanted to do was to use this as a chance to say something about sto-ries. These are very good examples of a pure story, and I talk about when a good one works, and why, and why that one doesn't work so well. Pull it apart in the middle and you can do this to it, and that to it, how they work better. I've taken liberties with quite a number of the stories and altered them and cut them a bit. Added to them a bit, turned them around.*

SAVING LIBRARIES

In many parts of England, local authorities have proposed funding cuts to libraries. Pullman lives in Oxfordshire, where the Oxfordshire County Council planned to stop funding nearly half of its forty-three libraries. Its solution to the funding problem was to ask volunteers to take over the operation of the libraries.

In a passionate speech in front of several hundred people at the Oxfordshire library campaigners' meeting, Pullman openly criticized the council and defended the role that libraries play in society. He said:

> I still remember the first library ticket I ever had. It must have been about 1957. My mother took me to the public library just off Battersea Park Road and enrolled me. I was thrilled. All those books, and I was allowed to borrow whichever I wanted! ... But what a gift to give a child, this chance to discover that you can love a book and the characters in it, you can become their friend and share their adventures in your own imagination. (as quoted by FalseEconomy.org).

On the council's suggestion that volunteers from the community run the libraries, Pullman was offended and delivered an angry response in defense of librarians. He directly addressed Keith Mitchell, the leader of the county council, saying:

Does he think the job of a librarian is so simple, so empty of content, that anyone can step up and do it for a thank-you and a cup of tea? Does he think that all a librarian does is to tidy the shelves? And who are these volun-teers? Who are these people whose lives are so empty, whose time spreads out in front of them like the limitless steppes of central Asia, who have no families to look after, no jobs to do, no responsibilities of any sort, and yet are so wealthy that they can commit hours of their time every week to working for noth-ing? Who are these volunteers? Do you know anyone who could volunteer their time in

Pullman is a great supporter of libraries. Here he participates in the unveiling of new gargoyles at the Bodleian Library at Oxford University, in England.

this way? If there's anyone who has the time and the energy to work for nothing in a good cause, they are probably already working for one of the voluntary sector day centers or running a local football [soccer] team or helping out with the league of friends in a hospital. What's going to make them stop doing that and start working in a library instead?

PHILIP PULLMAN QUOTES

Pullman has had a lot to say about a number of topics, from his own writing and storytelling to his beliefs about religion and education in Great Britain:

- "I am a storyteller. If I wanted to send a message, I would have written a sermon."
- "We don't need a list of rights and wrongs, tables of dos and don'ts: we need books, time, and silence. *Thou shalt not* is soon forgotten, but *Once upon a time* lasts forever."
- "After nourishment, shelter, and companionship, stories are the thing we need most in the world."
- "There's a hunger for stories in all of us, adults, too. We need stories so much that we're even willing to read bad books to get them, if the good books won't supply them."

- "As Jane Austen might have put it: It is a truth universally acknowledged that young protagonists in search of adventure must ditch their parents."
- "Writer's block is a condition that affects amateurs and people who aren't serious about writing. So is the opposite, namely inspiration, which amateurs are also very fond of. Putting it another way: a professional writer is someone who writes just as well when they're not inspired as when they are."
- "Children are not less intelligent than adults; what they are is less informed."
- "Imagination is a form of seeing."

Pullman's speech became a viral sensation, thanks to social media. When the speech was posted online, more than twenty thousand people read it in less than two days. Fans and fellow authors tweeted about the speech and rallied their support behind their local libraries. The speech was translated into French, and a number of events, called "read-ins," were scheduled at libraries throughout England.

STANDING UP FOR HUMAN RIGHTS

In 2010, Pullman, along with fifty-four other public figures, signed an open letter stating his opposition to Pope Benedict XVI, then the leader of the Catholic Church, visiting the United Kingdom. The letter was published in the *Guardian* newspaper. It argued that the Pope had led and/or condoned global abuses of human rights. A portion of the letter reads, "The state of which the pope is head has also resisted signing many major human rights treaties and has formed its own treaties with many states which negatively affect the human rights of citizens of those states."

In addition to Pullman's signature are those of Stephen Fry, an English actor and screenwriter; Richard Dawkins, an evolutionary biologist at New College, Oxford; Terry Pratchett, an

Pullman greets fans and signs books at the Oxford Literary Festival. Having been a teacher, Pullman is a staunch advocate for providing education to all children.

English author of fantasy novels; Jonathan Miller, a British theater and opera director; and Ken Follett, a Welsh author of thrillers and historical novels.

SUPPORTING EDUCATION REFORM

Having been a teacher for twenty years at both the middle school and university levels, Pullman has a well-developed opinion on education, particularly how stories are taught to children. He has criticized educators for the painful way that they have torn apart the great works of literature. He thinks that instead of being drilled and quizzed about these stories, children should be given time to enjoy them, to explore the world created by the book, and to find common ground with its characters. He told the newspaper the *Guardian*, "There should be plenty of books and plenty of time, and teachers should leave children alone."

In an essay he wrote for the *Guardian*, Pullman says it's a mistake to call things such as grammar and spelling "the basics" in teaching English. Instead, he says, teachers should focus on "teaching techniques that do work well...combining short sentences into longer ones, and embedding elements into simple sentences to make them more complex: in other words, using the language to say something."

Using the language to say something is what Philip Pullman has done so well and continues to do. Whether one agrees or disagrees with his ideas on religion and society, what is beyond dispute is the artistry of his use of the language, the power of his storytelling, and the enchantment of the worlds he creates and the characters he populates them with. He does indeed create a paradise for readers and dreamers of all ages, one that hopefully will never be lost.

ON PHILIP PULLMAN

Birth date: October 19, 1946

Birthplace: Norwich, England

Current residence: Oxford, England

First adult book publication: *The Haunted Storm* (1972)

First children's book publication: *Count Karlstein* (1982)

Marital status: Married to Judith Speller since 1970

Family: Two sons; one grandchild

Education: Exeter College, Oxford

Major awards: Carnegie Medal, Astrid Lindgren Memorial Award, *Guardian* Award, Nestlé Smarties Book Prize, Costa Book of the Year, 70th Anniversary Carnegie of Carnegies

Film/TV adaptations: *I Was a Rat!* (BBC miniseries; 2001); *The Butterfly Tattoo* (Dynamic Entertainment; 2009); *The Ruby in the Smoke* (BBC/WGBH; 2006); *The Shadow in the North* (BBC/WGBH; 2007); *The Golden Compass* (New Line Cinema; 2007)

ON PHILIP PULLMAN'S WORK

Non-Series Books

The Haunted Storm	1972

Joint winner of the New English Library's Young Writer's Award in 1972

Galatea	1976
Count Karlstein	1982

Pullman's first children's book to be published

How to Be Cool	1987

Adapted for television in the United Kingdom by Granada Television

Spring-Heeled Jack	1989
The Broken Bridge	1990
The White Mercedes (republished as *The Butterfly Tattoo*)	1992

Released as a feature length film in 2009

The Wonderful Story of Aladdin and the Enchanted Lamp	1993
Clockwork	1995

Twice adapted as an opera for children

The Firework-Maker's Daughter   1995
    Adapted as an opera
Mossycoat   1998
I Was a Rat! or *The Scarlet Slippers*   1999
    A three-part televised adaptation of
    the novel aired on the BBC in 2001
Puss in Boots: The Adventures of That
Most Enterprising Feline   2000
The Scarecrow and His Servant   2004
    Won the Nestlé Smarties Book
    Prize Silver Award in 2005
    Shortlisted for the 2004 Carnegie Medal
The Good Man Jesus and the Scoundrel
Christ   2010

Sally Lockhart series

The Ruby in the Smoke   1985
    Adapted for television in the United
    Kingdom in 2006
The Shadow in the North   1986
    Adapted for television in the United
    Kingdom in 2007
The Tiger in the Well   1990
    Adapted for television in the United
    Kingdom in 2007
The Tin Princess   1994
    Adapted for television in the United
    Kingdom in 2009

The New-Cut Gang series

Thunderbolt's Waxwork	1994
The Gasfitter's Ball	1995

His Dark Materials series

Entire series published in forty countries
All three books have been listed on the
best-sellers list of the *New York Times*,
the *Wall Street Journal*, the *San Francisco
Chronicle*, *Book Sense*, and *Publishers
Weekly.*
Northern Lights (retitled *The Golden Compass*
in the United States)   1995
    Won the Carnegie Medal for British
      children's books
    Won the *Guardian* Children's Fiction Prize
    Named *Booklist* Editors Choice–Top
      of the List
    Publishers Weekly Book of the Year
    Horn Book Fanfare Honor Book
    Bulletin Blue Ribbon Book
    Adapted for film by New Line Cinema
      (United States) and released to
      theaters in 2007; earned $70 million
      in U.S. box office; earned $53 million
      in the United Kingdom (second-
      highest-grossing, non-sequel film in
      United Kingdom)

In 2007, the judges of the CILIP Carnegie
Medal for children's literature selected the
book as one of the ten most important
children's novels of the previous seventy
years.

Won the Carnegie of Carnegies award

The Subtle Knife   1997

Parents' Choice Gold Book Award

American Library Association Best
  Book for Young Adults

Booklist Editors' Choice

Publishers Weekly Best Book of the Year

Horn Book Fanfare Honor Book

Bulletin Blue Ribbon Book

Book Links Best Book of the Year

American Bookseller Pick of the Lists

The Amber Spyglass   2000

Whitbread Book of the Year 2001

Named Children's Book of the Year at
  the 2001 British Book Awards

Long-listed for the Man Booker Prize

Companion Books

Lyra's Oxford (companion to *His Dark
Materials*)   2003

Once Upon a Time in the North (companion
to *His Dark Materials*)   2008

Northern Lights (retitled *The Golden Compass* in the United States) (1995)

"If you are the kind of reader who enjoys a book with big themes to ponder over, all set within an enthralling quest for Good against Evil, then you might like to try this book."—*Reading Matters, 2008*

"As always, Pullman is a master at combining impeccable characterizations and seamless plotting, maintaining a crackling pace to create scene upon scene of almost unbearable tension. This glittering gem will leave readers of all ages eagerly awaiting the next installment of Lyra's adventures."
—*Publishers Weekly, April 15, 1996*

"Pullman's fantasy masterpiece and the first of a trilogy . . . has become a classic of the genre."
—Billboard, August 14, 1999

The Subtle Knife (1997)

"*The Subtle Knife* is a fantasy adventure on the grand scale."—*Times Literary Supplement, December 10, 1999*

"More than fulfilling the promise of *The Golden Compass*, this second volume in the *His Dark Materials* trilogy starts off at a heart-thumping pace and never slows down." — *Publishers Weekly, July 21, 1997*

"*His Dark Materials*, by the English novelist Philip Pullman, is the latest trilogy to step up the pulse of kids and adults alike . . . Though this second volume almost succumbs to middle book syndrome, Pullman…avoids it, adroitly, by force of theme . . . J. R. R. Tolkien asserted that the best fantasy writing is marked by 'arresting strangeness.' Phillip Pullman measures up; his work is devilishly inventive … Put Philip Pullman on the shelf with Ursula K. LeGuin, Susan Cooper, Lloyd Alexander."—*New York Times Book Review, April 19, 1998*

The Amber Spyglass (2000)

"Almost everyone who does read Pullman becomes a fan."—*Newsweek, October 29, 2000*

"Rich in thought as well as adventure. Pullman knits religion, creation, evolution, death, physics, original sin, and growing up into his own personal theory of everything."—*U.S. News & World Report, October 23, 2000*

"In concluding the spellbinding *His Dark Materials* trilogy, Pullman produces what may well be the most controversial children's book of recent years …

Pullman riffs on the elemental chords of classical myth and fairytale. Stirring and highly provocative."
—*Publishers Weekly, May 19, 2003*

Fairy Tales from the Brother's Grimm (2012)
"*Fairy Tales from the Brothers Grimm* is mostly suited for people with a deep existing interest in classic fables, or in Pullman's personality, which periodically peeks up throughout the book. Those 'clear as water' versions do retain his authorial stamp, which is clearest in his entertainingly curt, judgmental author's notes."—*The A.V. Clu , December 31, 2012*

"Mr. Pullman's *Fairy Tales* offers something unique: the chance to watch a master storyteller think through these most foundational of tales."—*The New York Times, December 17, 2012*

"It is such a pleasure to read these tales again, to experience their strangeness and richness, their violence and beauty, their sheer nonsense . . . Reading Pullman's version, it is impossible not to hear Pullman's own gentle voice; he is present on every page ... [His] interventions work brilliantly."—*The Boston Globe, November 10, 2012*

"A real pleasure to read . . . This is the kind of writing that stands up to years of bedtime repetition . . .

The author's best appearances are in the notes, which are often as entertaining as the stories themselves . . . Swiftness and clarity, he says, were his guiding principles; to which he has added wit and invention . . . Beautiful or grotesque, the mad poetry of these tales is often delightfully funny too." — *The Economist, November 29, 2012*

"Excellent . . . His beginnings are like invitations that cannot be refused . . . Pullman shows how completely he understands the Grimms . . . [He] pays homage to the Brothers' pioneer work and simultaneously breathes new life into a great, venerable tradition of magical storytelling." — Jack Zipes, *Los Angeles Review of Books, November 12, 2012*

The Good Man Jesus and the Scoundrel Christ (2012)

"Though he wears his scholarship lightly as befits a master storyteller, there is no doubt in my mind that Pullman has a complete grasp of the intricacies of the quest for the historical Jesus." — *The Guardian, April 3, 2010*

"Both a perfect and perverse pairing: Philip Pullman and the 'myth' of Jesus Christ . . . It made me think of the story of Christ as just that: a great

story. At times, while reading, I had the pleasur-
able feeling of two versions of a tale, the original
and this one, unfolding at once . . . In other
words, I felt myself involved and implicated."
— *The Globe and Mail, August 23, 2012*

"A fierce and beautiful book which, like the parable of
the Grand Inquisitor in *The Brothers Karamazov*,
will move even those who disagree with it." — *The
Guardian, April 3, 2010*

"Told in simple, unadorned prose that is nonetheless
beautifully effective, *The Good Man Jesus and the
Scoundrel Christ* traces the familiar journey towards
the cross and makes it fresh . . . A brilliant new inter-
pretation that is also a thought-provoking reflection
on the process of how stories come into existence
and accrue their meanings." — *The Sunday Times
Review, April 1, 2010*

1946 Philip Pullman is born.

1953 Pullman's father is killed in a plane crash.

1968 Pullman graduates from Exeter College, Oxford.

1970 Marries Judith Speller; begins career as a teacher.

1972 Publishes his first book, *The Haunted Storm.*

1978 *Galatea*, an adult fantasy-fiction novel, is published.

1982 Publishes his first children's book, *Count Karlstein.*

1986 Publishes *The Ruby and the Smoke*; quits teaching middle school and accepts a lecturer position at Westminster College.

1993 The first book in *His Dark Materials* trilogy, *Northern Lights* (retitled *The Golden Compass* in the United States), is published.

1996 Quits teaching to write full-time.

1997 The second book in the *His Dark Materials* trilogy, *The Subtle Knife*, is published.

2000 The final book in the *His Dark Materials* trilogy, *The Amber Spyglass*, is published.

2003 Begins work on a companion book to *His Dark Materials*, *Lyra's Oxford.*

2005 Wins the biggest prize in children's literature, the Astrid Lindgren Memorial Award from the Swedish Arts Council.

2007 Film adaptation of *The Golden Compass* is released in international theaters.

2008 Publishes a second companion book to *His Dark Materials, Once Upon a Time in the North.*

2012 Begins writing *The Book of Dust*, a two-part companion series to *His Dark Materials*; is invited by Penguin Classics to "curate" fifty of Grimms' classic fairytales.

2013 *Fairy Tales from the Brothers Grimm* is published by Penguin Classics.

ADVOCATE One who pleads the cause of another.

AGNOSTIC One who is not committed to believing in either the existence or nonexistence of God or any gods.

APPRENTICE One who is learning, by practical experience and under skilled workers, a trade, art, or calling.

ATHEIST One who believes that there is no deity or God.

CELEBRITY A famous or celebrated person.

CLERIC A member of the clergy.

COLONY A body of people living in a new territory but retaining ties with the parent state.

COMIC BOOK A magazine containing sequences of comic strips and telling an extended story.

CONTROVERSY A discussion marked by the expression of opposing views; a dispute; a quarrel or strife.

CONVICTION A strong persuasion or belief.

CRYPTIC Having or seeming to have a hidden or mysterious meaning.

DAEMON A supernatural being of Greek mythology that is intermediate between gods and men.

DEBATE A regulated discussion of a proposition between two matched sides.

EXPLOIT A notable or heroic act or deed.

FANTASIA A free-form, usually instrumental composition; not abiding by a strict or rigid form;

something possessing grotesque, bizarre, or unreal qualities.

HEROINE A woman admired and emulated for her achievements and qualities.

HISTORICAL NOVEL A novel having as its setting a real and specific period of history.

INTRIGUE A secret scheme (noun); to get or accomplish something through the use of a secret scheme (verb); to arouse the interest or curiosity of (verb).

LECTURER A person who gives lectures, lessons, or other public instruction or speeches.

MELODRAMA A work characterized by extravagant theatricality and the emphasis of plot and action over characterization; having a sensational or theatrical quality.

MYTHOLOGY The myths dealing with the gods, demigods, and legendary heroes of a particular people.

PARTICLE A minute quantity or fragment; a relatively small or the smallest portion or amount of something; any of the basic units of matter and energy (such as molecule, atom, proton, electron, or photon).

PLOT The plan or main story of a novel, short story, play, film, or other narrative.

PUBLISHER A person or corporation whose business is publishing—the editing, printing, and distribution for sale of books.

RETROSPECTIVE Based on memory; relating to things in the past; backward looking.

SOAPBOX An improvised platform used by a self-appointed, spontaneous, or informal orator expressing a strong opinion about a public issue or question.

SQUADRON A unit of military organization.

TOMBOY A girl who behaves in a manner usually considered more typical of boys.

TOUCHSTONE A test or criterion for determining the quality or genuineness of a thing.

TRILOGY A series of three dramas or literary works that are closely related and develop a single theme, storyline, or narrative.

TYCOON A businessperson of exceptional wealth and power.

UNDERPRIVILEGED Deprived through one's social or economic condition of some of the fundamental rights of all members of a civilized society.

Alliance for Young Artists & Writers
557 Broadway
New York, NY 10012
Web site: http://www.artandwriting.org
The Alliance for Young Artists & Writers is a nonprofit
    organization that identifies teens with artistic and
    literary talent and showcases their work and pro-
    vides awards and scholarships.

Amazing Kids! Magazine
20126 Ballinger Way NE, Suite 239
Shoreline, WA 98155
(206) 331-3807
Web site: http://www.amazing-kids.org
This student-created online magazine and Web site
    is dedicated to helping young people realize their
    creative potential.

The Center for the Book
Library of Congress
101 Independence Avenue SE
Washington, DC 20540-4920
(202) 707-5221
Web site: http://www.read.gov/cfb
The Center for the Book was established by the
    Library of Congress and now exists in all fifty
    states to promote reading and literacy.

Children's Book Insider
901 Columbia Road
Fort Collins, CO 80525

(970) 495-0056
Web site: http://www.write4kids.com
This is a well-respected newsletter for children's
    writers.

Children's Literature Web Guide
Doucette Library of Teaching Resources
University of Calgary
Calgary, AB T2N 1N4
Canada
Web site: http://people.ucalgary.ca/~dkbrown/
The Children's Literature Web Guide gathers
    together and categorizes the growing number of
    Internet resources related to books for children
    and young adults.

DogEared
National Geographic Kids—Digital Media
1145 17th Street NW
Washington, DC 20036
This blog about books, with reviews, recommenda-
    tions, opinions, and wish lists is written by kids.

Kenyon Review Young Writers Workshop
Finn House
102 West Wiggin Street
Kenyon College
Gambier, OH 43022
(740) 427-5208
Young Writers is an intensive two-week workshop
    for intellectually curious, motivated high school

students who value writing. Its goal is to help students develop their creative and critical abilities with language to become better, more productive writers and more insightful thinkers. The program is sponsored by the *Kenyon Review*, one of the country's preeminent literary magazines.

National Writer's Association
10940 South Parker Road, #508
Parker, CO 80134
(303) 841-0246
Web site: http://www.nationalwriters.com
The National Writer's Association is a nonprofit organization that provides education and resources for writers of differing levels of experience.

Scholastic Art & Writing Awards
The Alliance for Young Artists and Writers
557 Broadway
New York, NY 10012
Web site: http://www.artandwriting.org
The Alliance for Young Artists & Writers, a nonprofit organization, identifies teenagers with exceptional artistic and literary talent and brings their work to a national audience through the Scholastic Art & Writing Awards.

Science Fiction and Fantasy Writers of America
P.O. Box 3238
Enfield, CT 06083-3238
Web site: http://www.sfwa.org

This is a professional organization for authors of science fiction, fantasy, and related genres.

Society of Children's Book Writers and Illustrators
8271 Beverly Boulevard
Los Angeles, CA 90048
(323) 782-1010
Web site: http://www.scbwi.org
This is one of the largest professional organizations for writers and illustrators and the only one specifically for those individuals writing and illustrating for children and young adults in the fields of children's literature, magazines, film, television, and multimedia.

Weekly Reader Publishing
Weekly Reader's Student Publishing Contest
3001 Cindel Drive
Delran, NJ 08075
(800) 446-3355
Web site: http://www.weeklyreadcr.com
Weekly Reader's Student Publishing Contest honors the nation's best nonfiction writing by students in grades 3 to 12. Individual pieces, as well as print and online student publications, are eligible. Winners receive a free trip to Washington, D.C., plus other prizes.

Young Author's Foundation
Teen Ink
P.O. Box 30

Newton, MA 02461
(617) 964-6800
Web site: http://www.teenink.com
Teen Ink is a national nonprofit teen magazine, book
series, and Web site that focuses on teen writing
and art. It is distributed through classrooms by
teachers.

WEB SITES

Due to the changing nature of Internet links, Rosen
Publishing has developed an online list of Web sites
related to the subject of this book. This site is updated
regularly. Please use this link to access the list:

http://www.rosenlinks.com/AAA/pull

FOR FURTHER READING

Anderson, Laurie Halse. *Speak*. New York, NY: Square Fish, 2011.

Clare, Cassandra. *The Mortal Instruments: City of Ashes* (Book 2). New York, NY: Margaret K. McElderry Books, 2009.

Clare, Cassandra. *The Mortal Instruments: City of Bones* (Book 1). New York, NY: Margaret K. McElderry Books, 2008.

Clare, Cassandra. *The Mortal Instruments: City of Fallen Angels* (Book 4). New York, NY: Margaret K. McElderry Books, 2012.

Clare, Cassandra. *The Mortal Instruments: City of Glass* (Book 3). New York, NY: Margaret K. McElderry Books, 2010.

Clare, Cassandra. *The Mortal Instruments: City of Lost Souls* (Book 5). New York, NY: Margaret K. McElderry Books, 2012.

Clare, Cassandra. *The Infernal Devices: Clockwork Angel* (Book 1). New York, NY: Margaret K. McElderry Books, 2011.

Clare, Cassandra. *The Infernal Devices: Clockwork Prince* (Book 2). New York, NY: Margaret K. McElderry Books, 2012.

Clare, Cassandra. *The Infernal Devices: Clockwork Princess* (Book 3). New York, NY: Margaret K. McElderry Books, 2013.

Collins, Suzanne. *Catching Fire*. New York, NY: Scholastic Press, 2009.

Collins, Suzanne. *The Hunger Games.* New York, NY: Scholastic Press, 2009.

Collins, Suzanne. *Mockingjay.* New York, NY: Scholastic Press, 2010.

de la Cruz, Melissa. *Bloody Valentine* (Blue Bloods, Book 7). New York, NY: Hyperion, 2010.

de la Cruz, Melissa. *Blue Bloods* (Blue Bloods, Book 1). New York, NY: Hyperion, 2007.

de la Cruz, Melissa. *Gates of Paradise* (Blue Bloods, Book 9). New York, NY: Hyperion, 2013.

de la Cruz, Melissa. *Keys to the Repository* (Blue Bloods, Book 5). New York, NY: Hyperion, 2010.

de la Cruz, Melissa. *Lost in Time* (Blue Bloods, Book 8). New York, NY: Hyperion, 2011.

de la Cruz, Melissa. *Masquerade* (Blue Bloods, Book 2). New York, NY: Hyperion, 2008.

de la Cruz, Melissa. *Misguided Angel* (Blue Bloods, Book 6). New York, NY: Hyperion, 2010.

de la Cruz, Melissa. *Revelations* (Blue Bloods, Book 3). New York, NY: Hyperion, 2007.

de la Cruz, Melissa. *The Van Alen Legacy* (Blue Bloods, Book 4). New York, NY: Hyperion, 2009.

Fitzpatrick, Becca. *Crescendo* (Hush Hush, Book 2). New York, NY: Simon & Schuster Books for Young Readers, 2012.

Fitzpatrick, Becca. *Finale* (Hush Hush, Book 4). New York, NY: Simon & Schuster Books for Young Readers, 2012.

Fitzpatrick, Becca. *Hush Hush* (Hush Hush, Book 1). New York, NY: Simon & Schuster Books for Young Readers, 2010.

Fitzpatrick, Becca. Silence (Hush Hush, Book 3). New York, NY: Simon & Schuster Books for Young Readers, 2013.

Gracia, Kami. *Beautiful Creatures.* New York, NY: Little, Brown Books for Young Readers, 2009.

Hocking, Amanda. *Lullaby.* New York, NY: St. Martin's Griffin, 2012.

Kate, Lauren. *Passion* (Fallen, Book 3). New York, NY: Delacorte Books for Young Readers, 2012.

Kate, Lauren. *Rapture* (Fallen, Book 1). New York, NY: Delacorte Books for Young Readers, 2012.

Kate, Lauren. *Torment* (Fallen, Book 2). New York, NY: Delacorte Books for Young Readers, 2011.

L'Engle, Madeleine. *Many Waters.* New York, NY: Square Fish, 2007.

L'Engle, Madeleine. *A Swiftly Tilting Planet.* New York, NY: Square Fish, 2007.

L'Engle, Madeleine. *A Wind in the Door.* New York, NY: Square Fish, 2007.

L'Engle, Madeleine. *A Wrinkle in Time.* New York, NY: FSG, 2012.

Meyer, Marissa. *Cinder.* New York, NY: Square Fish, 2012.

Milton, John. *Paradise Lost.* Seattle, WA: CreateSpace, 2013.

Roth, Veronica. *Divergent.* New York, NY: Katherine Tegen Books, 2012.

Skye, Obert. *Leven Thumps and the Eyes of the Want.* Salt Lake City, UT: Deseret Book, 2007.

Answers.com. "Gale Biographies of Children's Authors: Philip Pullman." Retrieved February 2013 (http://www.answers.com/topic/philip-pullman).

Barfield, Steven, and Katharine Cox. *Critical Perspectives on Philip Pullman's* His Dark Materials: *Essays on the Novels, the Film, and the Stage Productions.* Jefferson, NC: McFarland, 2011.

Barton, Laura. "Philip Pullman." *Guardian*, April 18, 2010. Retrieved April 2013 (http://www.guardian.co.uk/books/2010/apr/19/philip-pullman-interview-catholic-church).

Bookwitch. "Philip Pullman—'In the Books, I'm in Command." Retrieved April 2013 (http://bookwitch.wordpress.com/interviews/philip-pullman-in-the-books-im-in-command/).

Brown, Helen. "Page in the Life: Philip Pullman." *Telegraph*, October 17, 2011. Retrieved February 2013 (http://www.telegraph.co.uk/culture/books/authorinterviews/8824867/Page-in-the-Life-Philip-Pullman.html).

Butler, Robert. "Philip Pullman's Dark Arts." MoreIntelligentLife.com, December 2007. Retrieved January 2013 (http://moreintelligentlife.com/story/an-interview-with-philip-pullman).

Chattaway, Peter T. "Philip Pullman—The Extended Email Interview." Patheos.com, November 28, 2007. Retrieved April 2013 (http://www.patheos.com/blogs/filmchat/2007/11/philip-pullman-the-extended-e-mail-interview.html).

Edinger, Monica. "Interview: Philip Pullman on Retelling the Grimm Fairy Tales." Huffington Post, November

12, 2012. Retrieved April 2013 (http://www
.huffingtonpost.com/monica-edinger/the-brothers
-grimm_b_2163672.html).

Gribbin, Mary, and John Gribbin. *The Science of Philip
Pullman's* His Dark Materials. New York, NY: Knopf
Books for Young Readers, 2005.

Guardian. "Philip Pullman: A Life in Writing." March 3,
2011. Retrieved February 2013 (http://www.guardian
.co.uk/culture/2011/mar/03/philip-pullman-life-in
-writing).

Jones, Nicollette. "Interview: Philip Pullman on Grimm
Tales." *Telegraph*, October 3, 2012. Retrieved
January 2013 (http://www.telegraph.co.uk/culture/
books/bookreviews/9571067/Interview-Philip
-Pullman-on-Grimm-Tales.html).

KernelsCorner.com. "The Book of Dust: Beyond Philip
Pullman's *His Dark Materials*." Posted May 6, 2012.
Retrieved February 2013 (http://www.kernelscorner
.com/2012/05/book-of-dust-beyond-philip-pullmans
-his.html#.USJVTOh1H44).

Lacey, Hester. "The Inventory: Philip Pullman
Interview by Hester Lacey." PhilipPullman.com,
March 16, 2012. Retrieved April 2013 (http://www.
philip-pullman.com/pages/news/index
.asp?NewsID=76).

Lane, Harriet. "Pullman's Progress." *Guardian*, October
9, 2004. Retrieved January 2013 (http://www
.guardian.co.uk/books/2004/oct/10/
booksforchildrenandteenagers.philippullman).

McCrum, Robert. "Daemon Geezer." *Guardian*,
January 26, 2002. Retrieved February 2013

(http://www.guardian.co.uk/books/2002/jan/27/
whitbreadprize2001.costabookaward).

Mechanic, Michael. "His Grimm Materials: A
Conversation with Philip Pullman." *Mother Jones*,
November 2012. Retrieved February 2013 (http://
www.motherjones.com/media/2012/11/interview
-philip-pullman-grimm-fairy-tales-his-dark-materials).

Miller, Laura. "Far From Narnia: Philip Pullman's Secular
Fantasy for Children." *The New Yorker*, December
26, 2005. Retrieved February 2013 (http://www
.newyorker.com/archive/2005/12/26/051226fa_fact).

Mitchison, Amanda. "The Art of Darkness." *Telegraph*,
November 3, 2003. Retrieved February 14, 2013
(http://www.telegraph.co.uk/culture/donotmigrate/
3605857/The-art-of-darkness.html).

NBC News. "Pullman Not Promoting Atheism in 'Golden
Compass.'" November 2, 2007. Retrieved February
2013 (http://www.nbcnews.com/id/21595083/site/
todayshow/ns/today-books/t/pullman-not-promoting
-atheism-golden-compass/#.USJXEuh1H44).

NPR.org. "Philip Pullman Rewrites the Brothers
Grimm." November 6, 2012. Retrieved April 2013
(http://www.npr.org/2012/11/11/164432853/
philip-pullman-rewriting-the-brothers-grimm).

Pullman, Philip. "Common Sense Has Much to Learn
from Moonshine." *Guardian*, January 22, 2005.
Retrieved February 2013 (http://www.guardian
.co.uk/education/2005/jan/22/schools
.wordsandlanguage).

Pullman, Philip. "Leave Libraries Alone. You Don't
Understand Their Value." FalseEconomy.org,

January 20, 2011. Retrieved February 2013
(http://falseeconomy.org.uk/blog/save-oxfordshire
-libraries-speech-philip-pullman).

Pullman, Philip. "Philip Pullman Interview Transcript."
Scholastic.com. Retrieved January 2013
(http://www.scholastic.com/teachers/article/
philip-pullman-interview-transcript).

Rodcorp. "How We Work: Philip Pullman, Author."
December 30, 2007. Retrieved February 2013
(http://rodcorp.typepad.com/rodcorp/2007/12/how
-we-work-phi.html).

Squires, Claire. *Philip Pullman, Master Storyteller: A
Guide to the Worlds of* His Dark Materials. New
York, NY: Continuum, 2006.

Telegraph. "The Dark Materials Debate: Life, God, the
universe…" March 17, 2004. Retrieved April 2013
(http://www.telegraph.co.uk/culture/3613962/
The-Dark-Materials-debate-life-God-the
-universe....html).

Watkins, Tony. *Dark Matter: A Thinking Fan's Guide to
Philip Pullman.* Southhampton, England: Damaris
Trust, 2012.

Wheat, Leonard F. *Philip Pullman's HIS DARK
MATERIALS: A Multiple Allegory Attacking
Religious Superstition in* The Lion, the Witch, and
the Wardrobe *and* Paradise Lost. Amherst, NY:
Prometheus Books, 2007.

Wired.com. "Philip Pullman is planning on going
silent." December 27, 2012. Retrieved April 2013
(http://www.wired.com/underwire/2012/12/
geeks-guide-philip-pullman/).

ABOUT THE AUTHOR

Laura La Bella has written numerous biographies of public figures and pop culture celebrities, including Angelina Jolie, Carrie Underwood, Kanye West, Carl Edwards, and My Chemical Romance. She lives in Rochester, New York, with her husband and son.

PHOTO CREDITS

Cover, pp. 3, 6–7 David Levenson/Getty Images; p. 11 Popperfoto/Getty Images; p. 14 PRNewsFoto/Heritage Auctions/AP Images; p. 18 Universal Images Group/Getty Images; pp. 22–23, 44–45, 54 MJ Kim/Getty Images; p. 25 Dylan Martinez/Reuters/Landov; pp. 26–27 David Borland/View Pictures/Newscom; pp. 32–33 English School/Private Collection/Ken Walsh/The Bridgeman Art Library; p. 36 Peter Willi/SuperStock/Getty Images; pp. 40–41, 56–57 © Entertainment Pictures/ZUMA Press; pp. 47, 48 Sion Touhig/Getty Images; pp. 58–59 Steve Parsons/PA Photos/Landov; p. 63 Writers Pictures/AP Images; p. 69 Hulton Archive/Getty Images; p. 71 ZU_09/E+/Getty Images; pp. 74–75 Camera Press/Graham Wiltshire/Redux; pp. 78–79 Camera Press/Ian Lloyd/Redux; cover and interior pages background (marbleized texture) javarman/Shutterstock.com; cover and interior pages (book) www.iStockphoto.com/Andrzej Tokarski; interior pages background (landscape) © iStockphoto.com/Sava Alexandru.

Designer: Nicole Russo;
Photo Researcher: Karen Huang